MONTH

WEEK NO.

MONDAY

TUESDAY

WEDNESDAY

THURSDAY

FRIDAY

SATURDAY

SUNDAY

NOTES

I AM THANKFUL FOR..DATE............

I AM THANKFUL FOR..DATE............

I AM THANKFUL FOR..DATE............

I AM THANKFUL FOR..DATE............

I AM THANKFUL FOR..DATE............

I AM THANKFUL FOR..DATE............

QUOTE OR HIGHLIGHT OF THE WEEK

I AM THANKFUL FOR .... DATE ....

I AM THANKFUL FOR .... DATE ....

I AM THANKFUL FOR .... DATE ....

I AM THANKFUL FOR .... DATE ....

I AM THANKFUL FOR .... DATE ....

I AM THANKFUL FOR .... DATE ....

QUOTE OR HIGHLIGHT OF THE WEEK ....

I AM THANKFUL FOR..DATE..........
....
....

I AM THANKFUL FOR..DATE..........
....
....

I AM THANKFUL FOR..DATE..........
....
....

I AM THANKFUL FOR..DATE..........
....
....

I AM THANKFUL FOR..DATE..........
....
....

I AM THANKFUL FOR..DATE..........
....
....

QUOTE OR HIGHLIGHT OF THE WEEK..
....
....
....
....

I AM THANKFUL FOR...DATE..............

I AM THANKFUL FOR...DATE..............

I AM THANKFUL FOR...DATE..............

I AM THANKFUL FOR...DATE..............

I AM THANKFUL FOR...DATE..............

I AM THANKFUL FOR...DATE..............

QUOTE OR HIGHLIGHT OF THE WEEK..

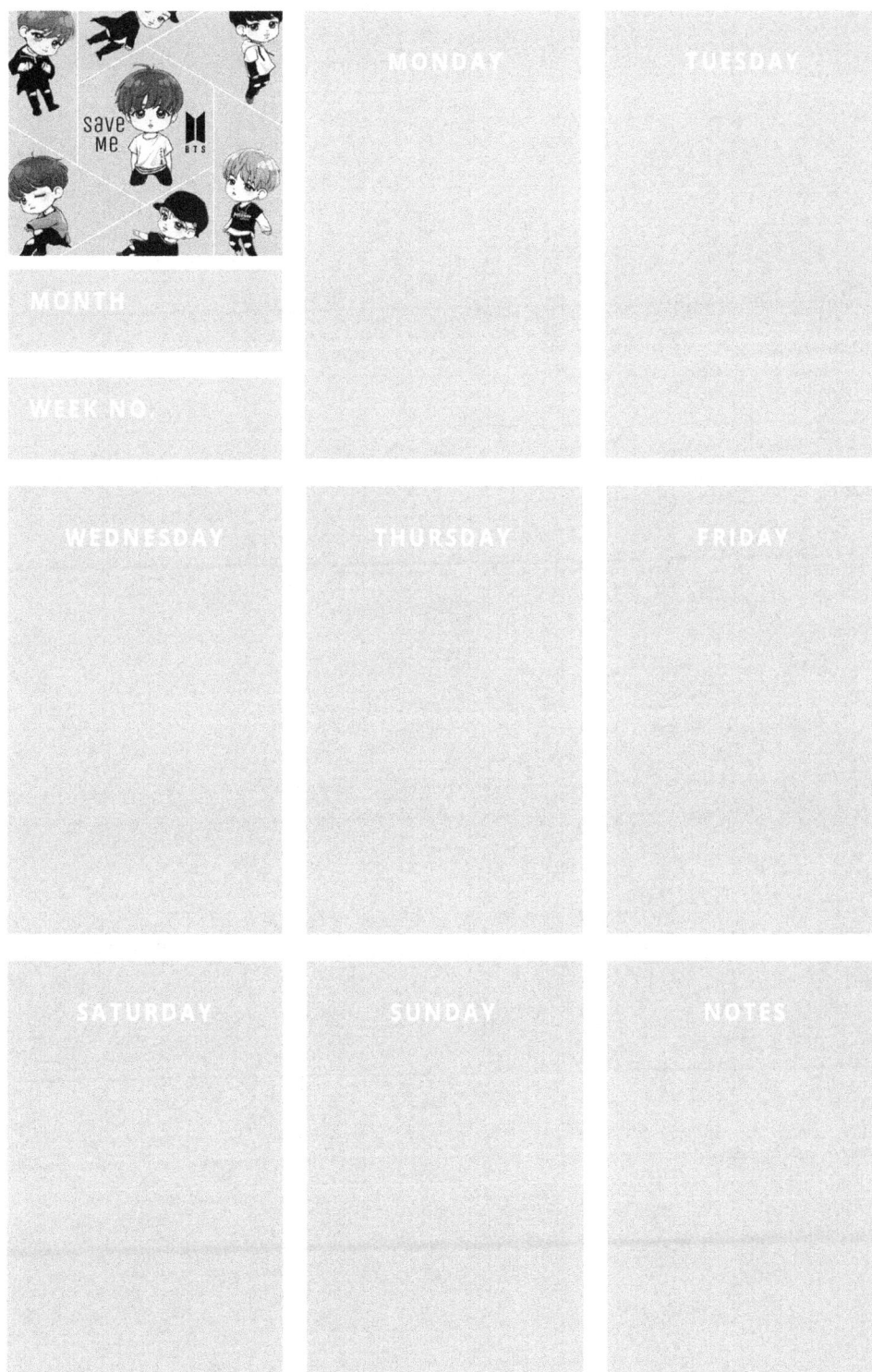

MONTH

WEEK NO.

MONDAY

TUESDAY

WEDNESDAY

THURSDAY

FRIDAY

SATURDAY

SUNDAY

NOTES

I AM THANKFUL FOR..DATE............
....
I AM THANKFUL FOR..DATE............
....
I AM THANKFUL FOR..DATE............
....
I AM THANKFUL FOR..DATE............
....
I AM THANKFUL FOR..DATE............
....
I AM THANKFUL FOR..DATE............
....

QUOTE OR HIGHLIGHT OF THE WEEK..
....
....

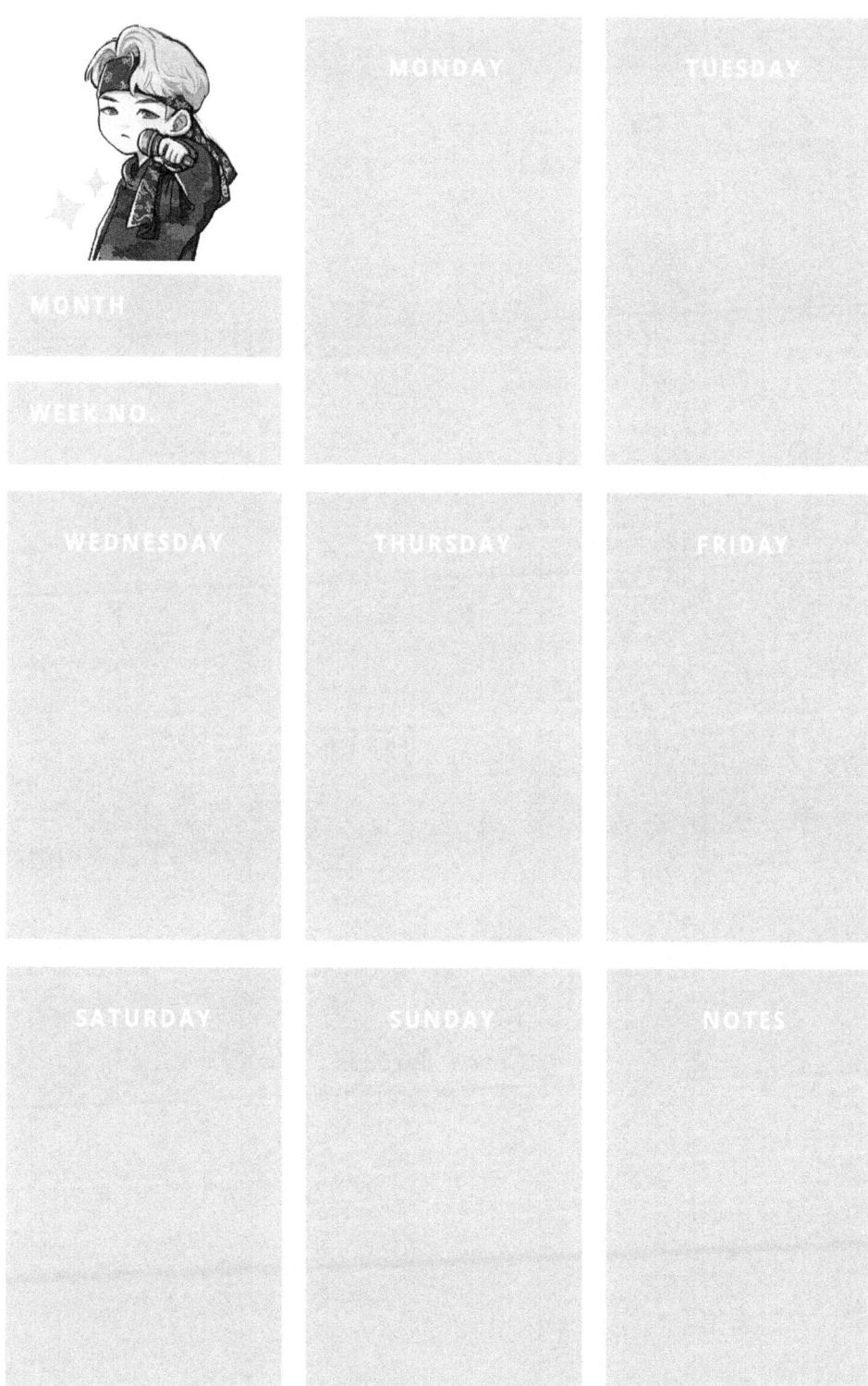

MONTH

WEEK NO.

MONDAY

TUESDAY

WEDNESDAY

THURSDAY

FRIDAY

SATURDAY

SUNDAY

NOTES

I AM THANKFUL FOR	DATE

well COME BACK!!!

I AM THANKFUL FOR	DATE

I AM THANKFUL FOR	DATE

I AM THANKFUL FOR	DATE

I AM THANKFUL FOR	DATE

I AM THANKFUL FOR	DATE

QUOTE OR HIGHLIGHT OF THE WEEK

| I AM THANKFUL FOR | DATE |

| I AM THANKFUL FOR | DATE |

| I AM THANKFUL FOR | DATE |

| I AM THANKFUL FOR | DATE |

| I AM THANKFUL FOR | DATE |

| I AM THANKFUL FOR | DATE |

QUOTE OR HIGHLIGHT OF THE WEEK

I AM THANKFUL FOR..DATE..........

I AM THANKFUL FOR..DATE..........

I AM THANKFUL FOR..DATE..........

I AM THANKFUL FOR..DATE..........

I AM THANKFUL FOR..DATE..........

I AM THANKFUL FOR..DATE..........

QUOTE OR HIGHLIGHT OF THE WEEK..

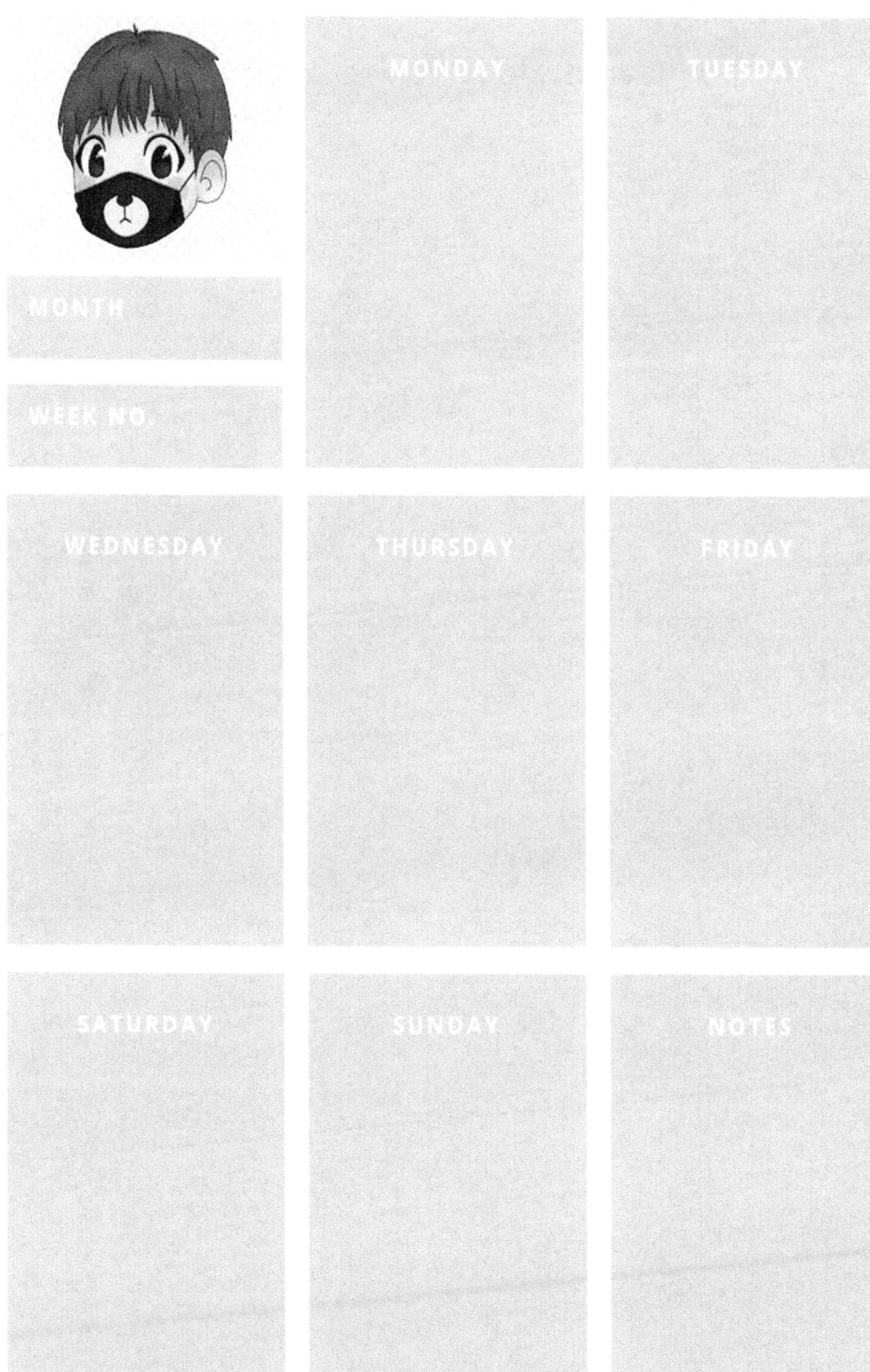

I AM THANKFUL FOR..DATE................

I AM THANKFUL FOR..DATE................

I AM THANKFUL FOR..DATE................

I AM THANKFUL FOR..DATE................

I AM THANKFUL FOR..DATE................

I AM THANKFUL FOR..DATE................

QUOTE OR HIGHLIGHT OF THE WEEK..

I AM THANKFUL FOR	DATE

I AM THANKFUL FOR	DATE

I AM THANKFUL FOR	DATE

I AM THANKFUL FOR	DATE

I AM THANKFUL FOR	DATE

I AM THANKFUL FOR	DATE

QUOTE OR HIGHLIGHT OF THE WEEK

I AM THANKFUL FOR...DATE...............

I AM THANKFUL FOR...DATE...............

I AM THANKFUL FOR...DATE...............

I AM THANKFUL FOR...DATE...............

I AM THANKFUL FOR...DATE...............

I AM THANKFUL FOR...DATE...............

QUOTE OR HIGHLIGHT OF THE WEEK..

BTS

I AM THANKFUL FOR..DATE..........

I AM THANKFUL FOR..DATE..........

I AM THANKFUL FOR..DATE..........

I AM THANKFUL FOR..DATE..........

I AM THANKFUL FOR..DATE..........

I AM THANKFUL FOR..DATE..........

QUOTE OR HIGHLIGHT OF THE WEEK.....................................

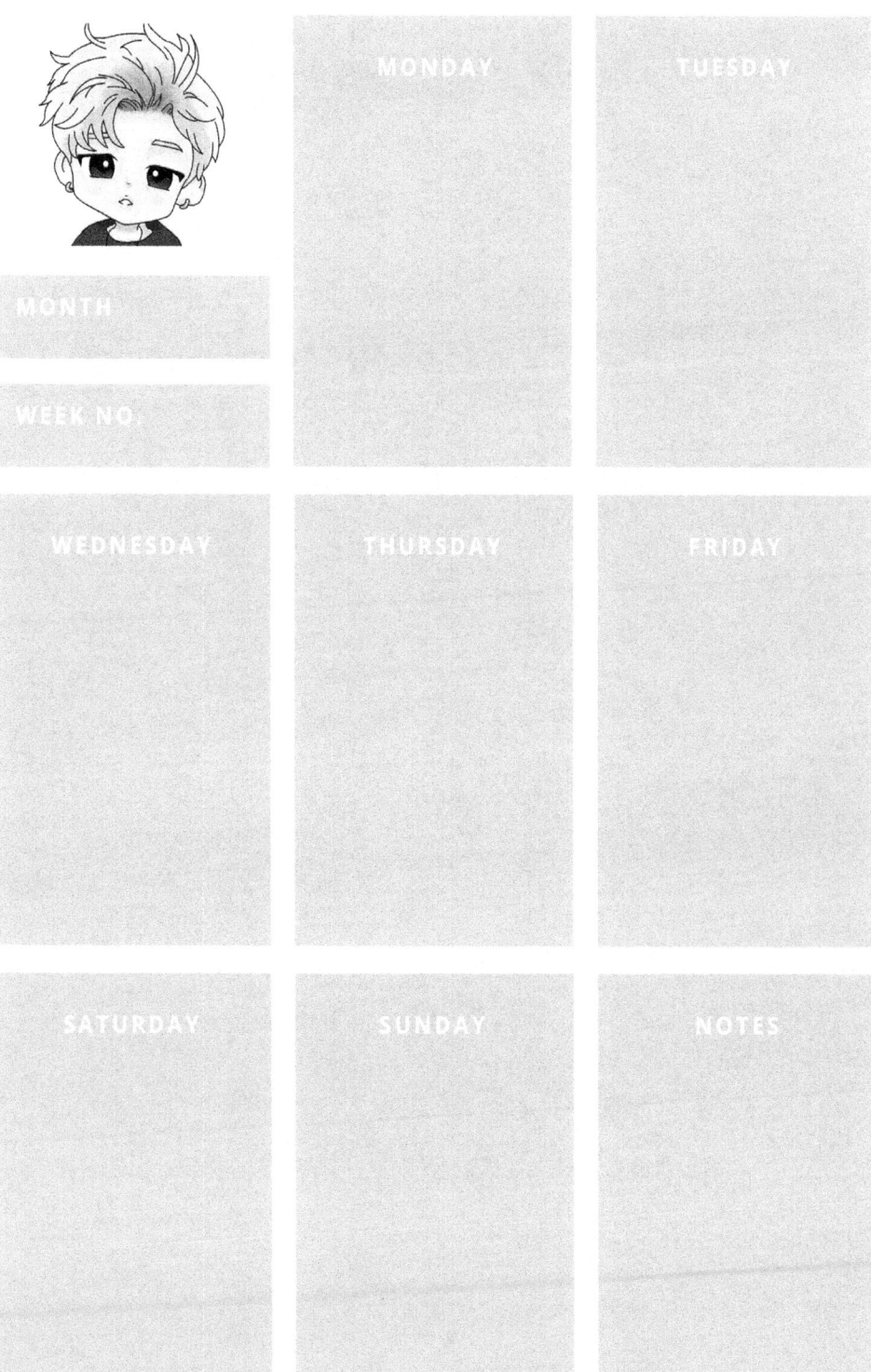

I AM THANKFUL FOR..DATE........

I AM THANKFUL FOR..DATE........

I AM THANKFUL FOR..DATE........

I AM THANKFUL FOR..DATE........

I AM THANKFUL FOR..DATE........

I AM THANKFUL FOR..DATE........

QUOTE OR HIGHLIGHT OF THE WEEK..

MONTH

WEEK NO.

MONDAY

TUESDAY

WEDNESDAY

THURSDAY

FRIDAY

SATURDAY

SUNDAY

NOTES

I AM THANKFUL FOR..DATE..........

I AM THANKFUL FOR..DATE..........

I AM THANKFUL FOR..DATE..........

I AM THANKFUL FOR..DATE..........

I AM THANKFUL FOR..DATE..........

I AM THANKFUL FOR..DATE..........

QUOTE OR HIGHLIGHT OF THE WEEK..

MONTH

WEEK NO.

MONDAY

TUESDAY

WEDNESDAY

THURSDAY

FRIDAY

SATURDAY

SUNDAY

NOTES

I AM THANKFUL FOR..DATE.............
....
....

I AM THANKFUL FOR..DATE.............
....
....

I AM THANKFUL FOR..DATE.............
....
....

I AM THANKFUL FOR..DATE.............
....
....

I AM THANKFUL FOR..DATE.............
....
....

I AM THANKFUL FOR..DATE.............
....
....

QUOTE OR HIGHLIGHT OF THE WEEK...
....
....
....

MONTH

WEEK NO.

MONDAY

TUESDAY

WEDNESDAY

THURSDAY

FRIDAY

SATURDAY

SUNDAY

NOTES

I AM THANKFUL FOR..DATE..............

BTS ♥

I AM THANKFUL FOR..DATE..............

I AM THANKFUL FOR..DATE..............

I AM THANKFUL FOR..DATE..............

I AM THANKFUL FOR..DATE..............

I AM THANKFUL FOR..DATE..............

QUOTE OR HIGHLIGHT OF THE WEEK..

I AM THANKFUL FOR .... DATE ....
....
....
....

I AM THANKFUL FOR .... DATE ....
....
....
....

I AM THANKFUL FOR .... DATE ....
....
....
....

I AM THANKFUL FOR .... DATE ....
....
....
....

I AM THANKFUL FOR .... DATE ....
....
....
....

I AM THANKFUL FOR .... DATE ....
....
....
....

QUOTE OR HIGHLIGHT OF THE WEEK ....
....
....
....
....
....
....

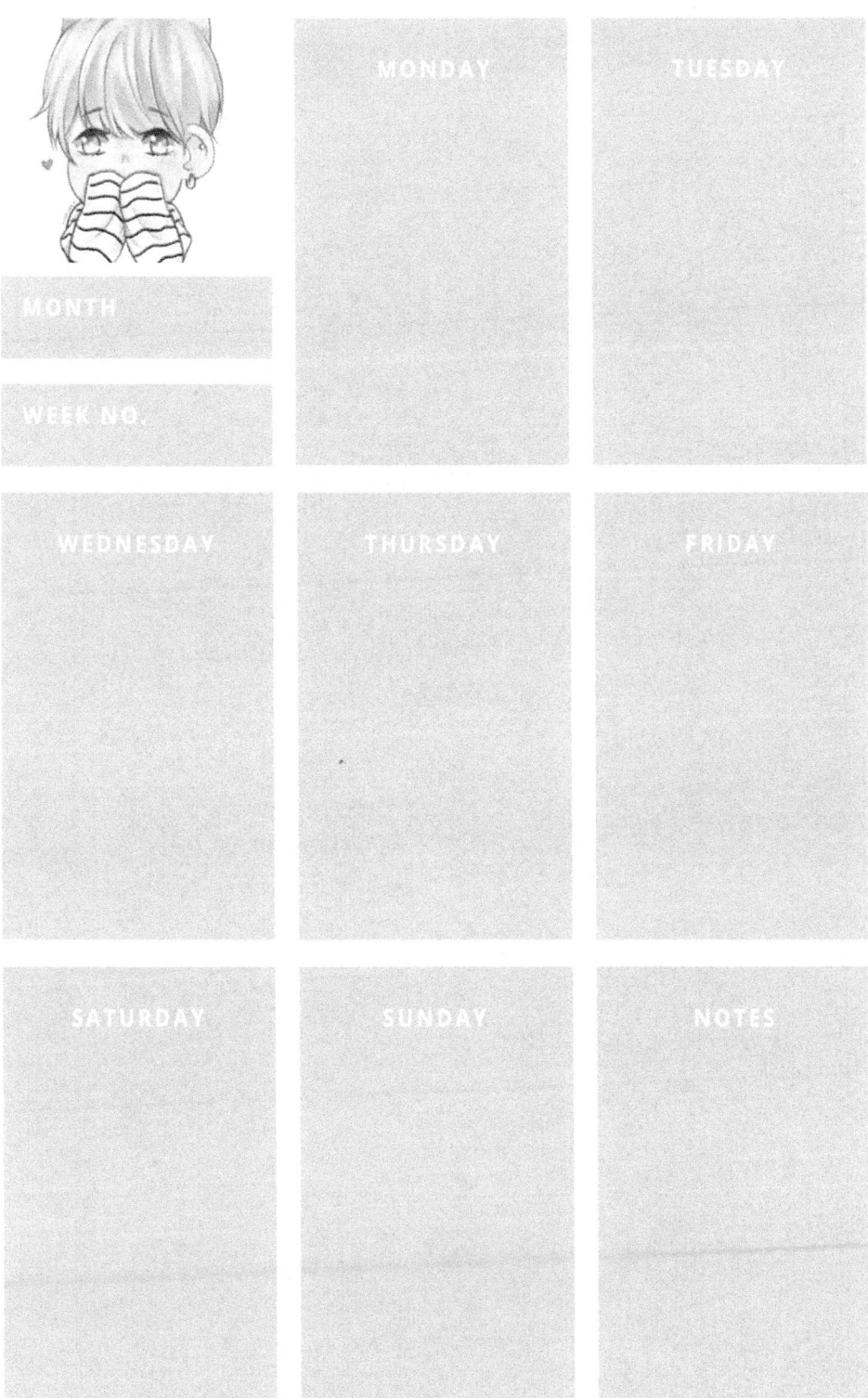

I AM THANKFUL FOR .... DATE ....
....
....

I AM THANKFUL FOR .... DATE ....
....
....

I AM THANKFUL FOR .... DATE ....
....
....

I AM THANKFUL FOR .... DATE ....
....
....

I AM THANKFUL FOR .... DATE ....
....
....

I AM THANKFUL FOR .... DATE ....
....
....

QUOTE OR HIGHLIGHT OF THE WEEK ....
....
....
....
....

MONTH

WEEK NO.

MONDAY

TUESDAY

WEDNESDAY

THURSDAY

FRIDAY

SATURDAY

SUNDAY

NOTES

I AM THANKFUL FOR......... DATE.........

BTS ♥

I AM THANKFUL FOR......... DATE.........

I AM THANKFUL FOR......... DATE.........

I AM THANKFUL FOR......... DATE.........

I AM THANKFUL FOR......... DATE.........

I AM THANKFUL FOR......... DATE.........

QUOTE OR HIGHLIGHT OF THE WEEK.........

MONTH

WEEK NO.

MONDAY

TUESDAY

WEDNESDAY

THURSDAY

FRIDAY

SATURDAY

SUNDAY

NOTES

I AM THANKFUL FOR...DATE..............

I AM THANKFUL FOR...DATE..............

I AM THANKFUL FOR...DATE..............

I AM THANKFUL FOR...DATE..............

I AM THANKFUL FOR...DATE..............

I AM THANKFUL FOR...DATE..............

QUOTE OR HIGHLIGHT OF THE WEEK................................

NOT TODAY

MONTH

WEEK NO.

MONDAY

TUESDAY

WEDNESDAY

THURSDAY

FRIDAY

SATURDAY

SUNDAY

NOTES

I AM THANKFUL FOR...DATE..................
....
....

I AM THANKFUL FOR...DATE..................
....
....

I AM THANKFUL FOR...DATE..................
....
....

I AM THANKFUL FOR...DATE..................
....
....

I AM THANKFUL FOR...DATE..................
....
....

I AM THANKFUL FOR...DATE..................
....
....

QUOTE OR HIGHLIGHT OF THE WEEK..
....
....
....

MONTH

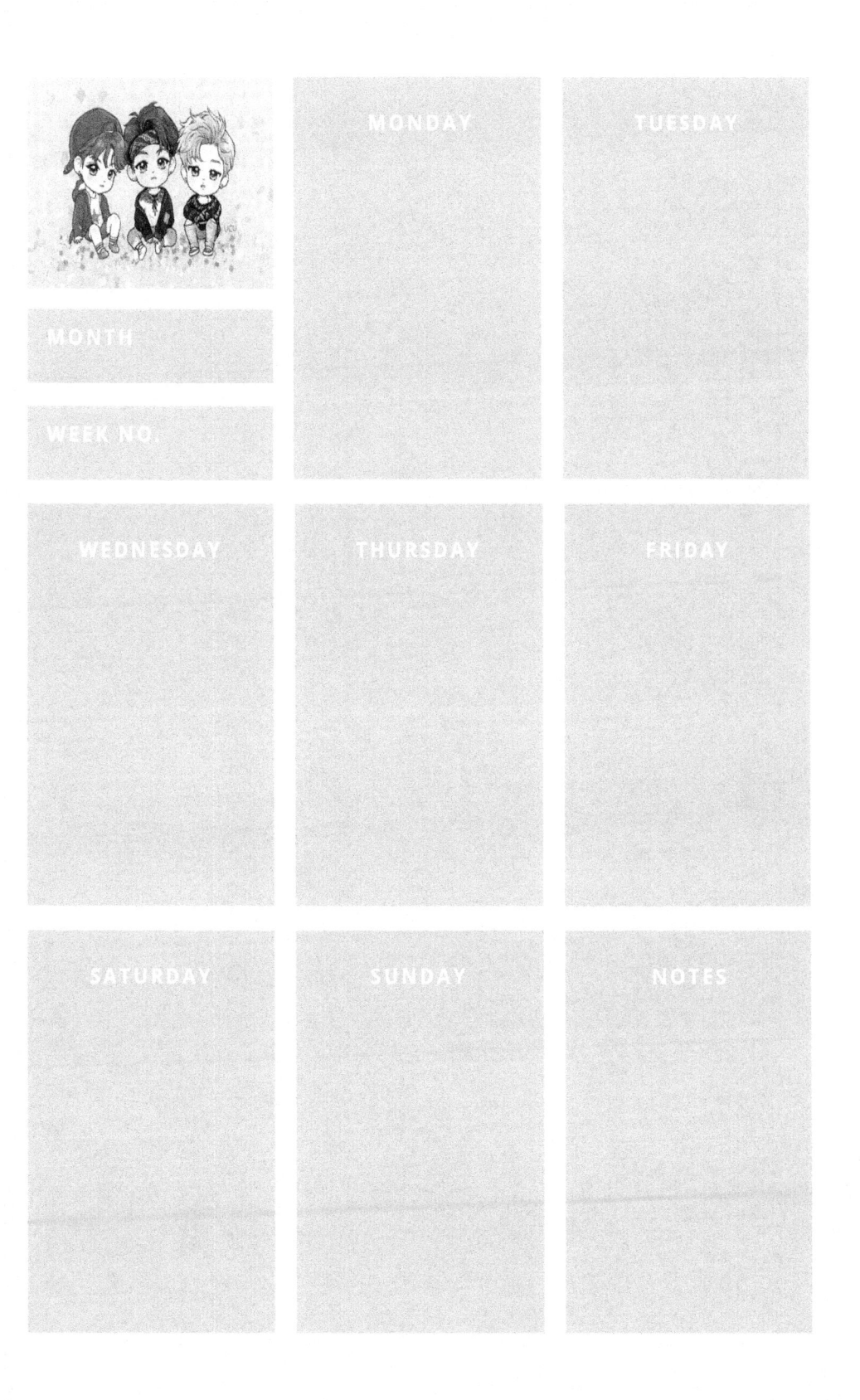

WEEK NO.

MONDAY

TUESDAY

WEDNESDAY

THURSDAY

FRIDAY

SATURDAY

SUNDAY

NOTES

I AM THANKFUL FOR..DATE............

I AM THANKFUL FOR..DATE............

I AM THANKFUL FOR..DATE............

I AM THANKFUL FOR..DATE............

I AM THANKFUL FOR..DATE............

I AM THANKFUL FOR..DATE............

QUOTE OR HIGHLIGHT OF THE WEEK

TOMATO

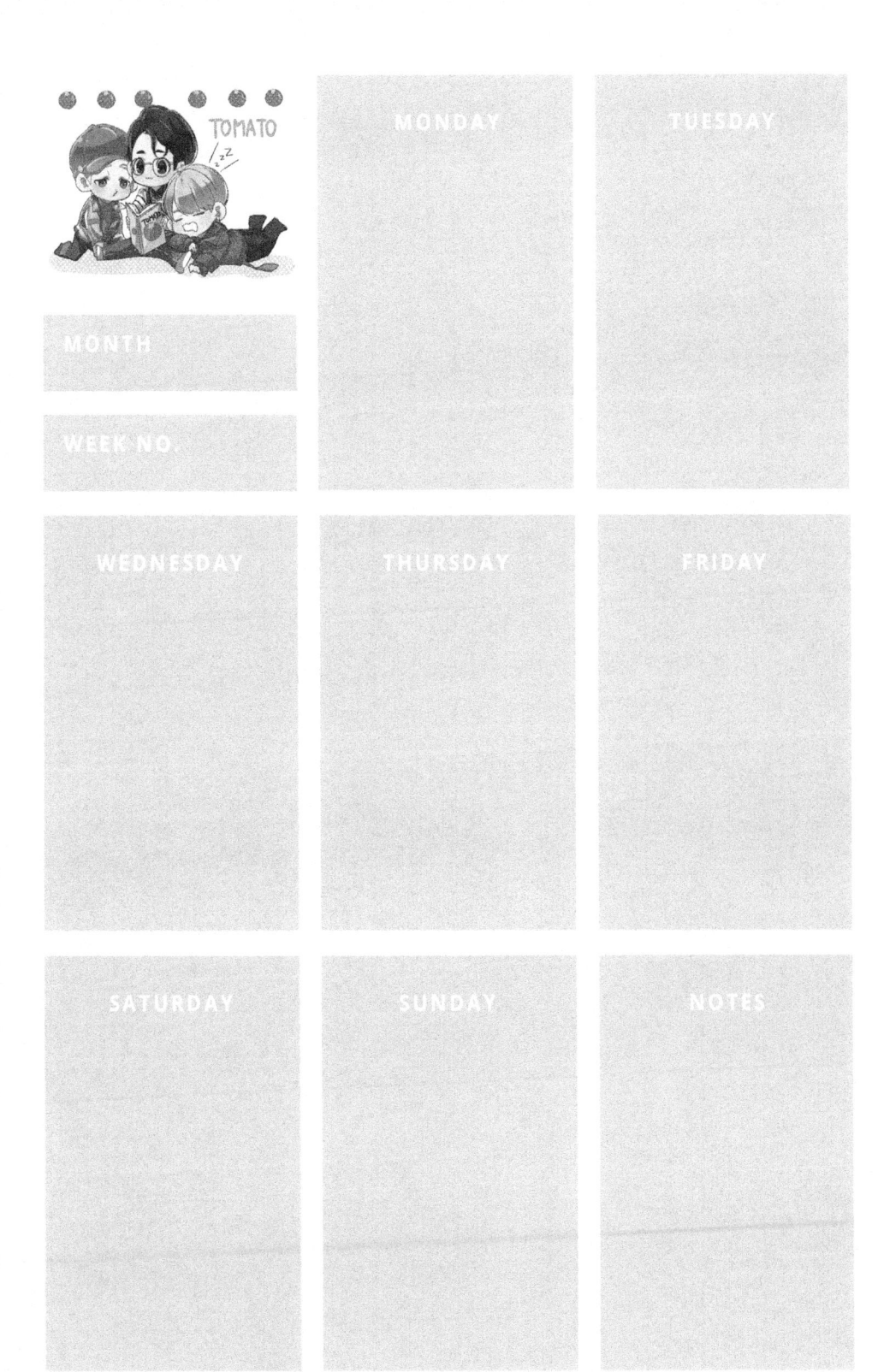

MONTH

WEEK NO.

MONDAY

TUESDAY

WEDNESDAY

THURSDAY

FRIDAY

SATURDAY

SUNDAY

NOTES

I AM THANKFUL FOR..DATE................

I AM THANKFUL FOR..DATE................

I AM THANKFUL FOR..DATE................

I AM THANKFUL FOR..DATE................

I AM THANKFUL FOR..DATE................

I AM THANKFUL FOR..DATE................

QUOTE OR HIGHLIGHT OF THE WEEK..................................

MONTH

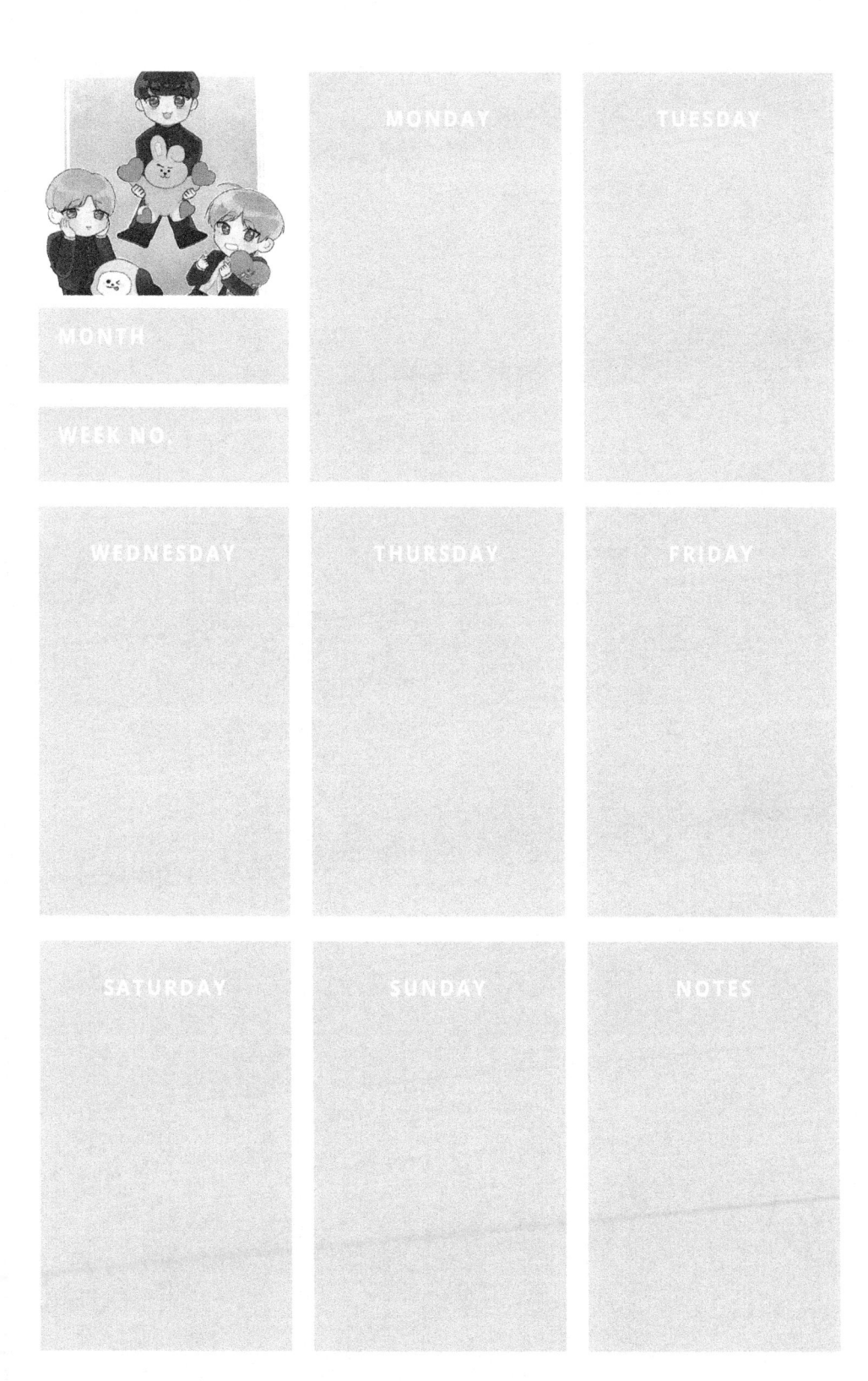

WEEK NO.

MONDAY

TUESDAY

WEDNESDAY

THURSDAY

FRIDAY

SATURDAY

SUNDAY

NOTES

I AM THANKFUL FOR..DATE...............
....
....

I AM THANKFUL FOR..DATE...............
....
....

I AM THANKFUL FOR..DATE...............
....
....

I AM THANKFUL FOR..DATE...............
....
....

I AM THANKFUL FOR..DATE...............
....
....

I AM THANKFUL FOR..DATE...............
....
....

QUOTE OR HIGHLIGHT OF THE WEEK..
....
....
....
....

MONTH

WEEK NO.

MONDAY

TUESDAY

WEDNESDAY

THURSDAY

FRIDAY

SATURDAY

SUNDAY

NOTES

BTS

I AM THANKFUL FOR .... DATE ....
....
....

I AM THANKFUL FOR .... DATE ....
....
....

I AM THANKFUL FOR .... DATE ....
....
....

I AM THANKFUL FOR .... DATE ....
....
....

I AM THANKFUL FOR .... DATE ....
....
....

I AM THANKFUL FOR .... DATE ....
....
....

QUOTE OR HIGHLIGHT OF THE WEEK ....
....
....
....
....
....

MAP OF THE SOUL
7

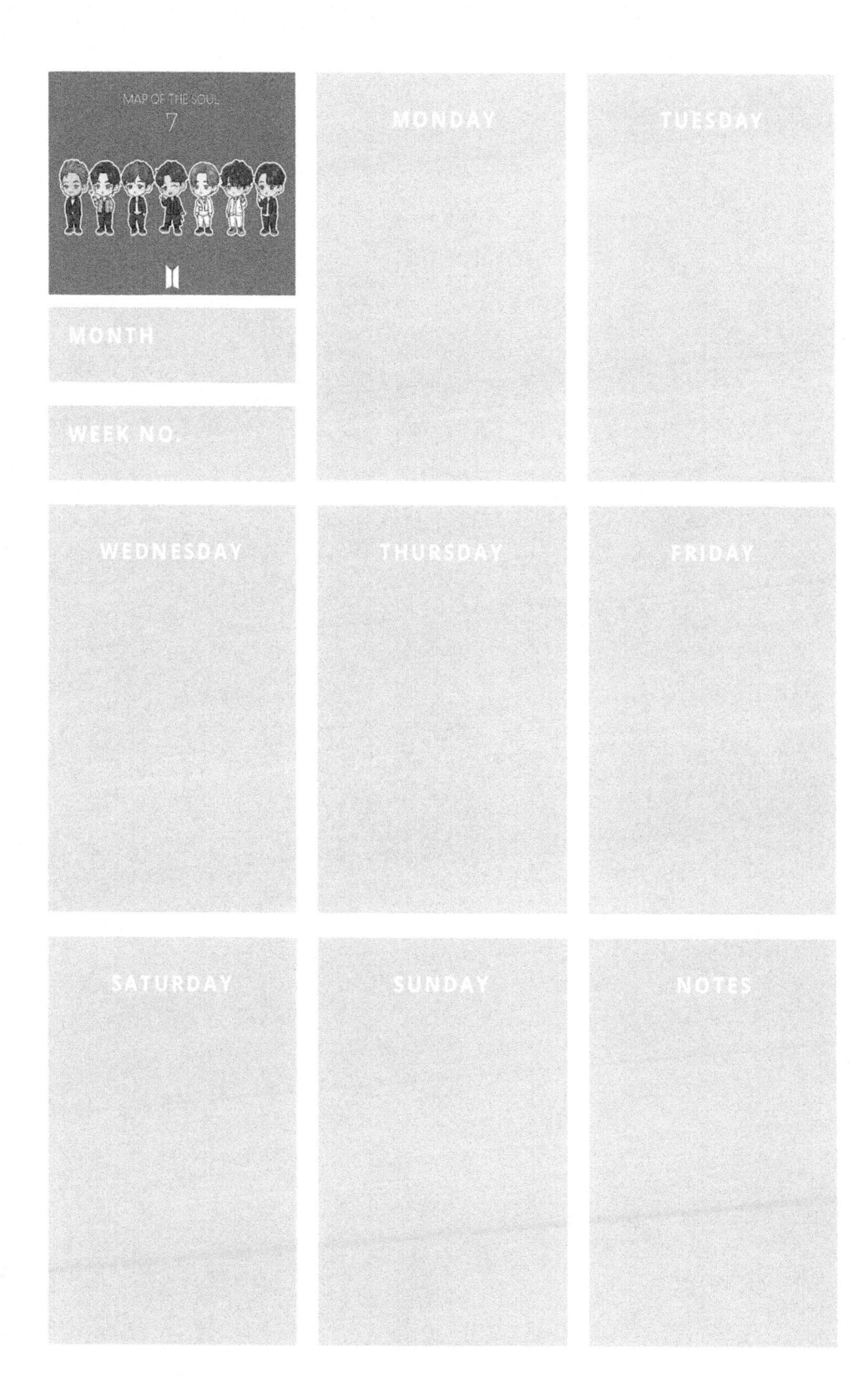

MONTH

WEEK NO.

MONDAY

TUESDAY

WEDNESDAY

THURSDAY

FRIDAY

SATURDAY

SUNDAY

NOTES

I AM THANKFUL FOR........ DATE........

I AM THANKFUL FOR........ DATE........

I AM THANKFUL FOR........ DATE........

I AM THANKFUL FOR........ DATE........

I AM THANKFUL FOR........ DATE........

I AM THANKFUL FOR........ DATE........

QUOTE OR HIGHLIGHT OF THE WEEK........

MONTH

WEEK NO.

MONDAY

TUESDAY

WEDNESDAY

THURSDAY

FRIDAY

SATURDAY

SUNDAY

NOTES

I AM THANKFUL FOR	DATE

I AM THANKFUL FOR	DATE

I AM THANKFUL FOR	DATE

I AM THANKFUL FOR	DATE

I AM THANKFUL FOR	DATE

I AM THANKFUL FOR	DATE

QUOTE OR HIGHLIGHT OF THE WEEK

MONTH

WEEK NO.

MONDAY

TUESDAY

WEDNESDAY

THURSDAY

FRIDAY

SATURDAY

SUNDAY

NOTES

I AM THANKFUL FOR..DATE..........

I AM THANKFUL FOR..DATE..........

I AM THANKFUL FOR..DATE..........

I AM THANKFUL FOR..DATE..........

I AM THANKFUL FOR..DATE..........

I AM THANKFUL FOR..DATE..........

QUOTE OR HIGHLIGHT OF THE WEEK...

MONTH

WEEK NO.

MONDAY

TUESDAY

WEDNESDAY

THURSDAY

FRIDAY

SATURDAY

SUNDAY

NOTES

I AM THANKFUL FOR...DATE...............

I AM THANKFUL FOR...DATE...............

I AM THANKFUL FOR...DATE...............

I AM THANKFUL FOR...DATE...............

I AM THANKFUL FOR...DATE...............

I AM THANKFUL FOR...DATE...............

QUOTE OR HIGHLIGHT OF THE WEEK..

MONTH

WEEK NO.

MONDAY

TUESDAY

WEDNESDAY

THURSDAY

FRIDAY

SATURDAY

SUNDAY

NOTES

I AM THANKFUL FOR... ... DATE...

I AM THANKFUL FOR... ... DATE...

I AM THANKFUL FOR... ... DATE...

I AM THANKFUL FOR... ... DATE...

I AM THANKFUL FOR... ... DATE...

I AM THANKFUL FOR... ... DATE...

QUOTE OR HIGHLIGHT OF THE WEEK...

MONTH

WEEK NO.

MONDAY

TUESDAY

WEDNESDAY

THURSDAY

FRIDAY

SATURDAY

SUNDAY

NOTES

I AM THANKFUL FOR..DATE..........

I AM THANKFUL FOR..DATE..........

I AM THANKFUL FOR..DATE..........

I AM THANKFUL FOR..DATE..........

I AM THANKFUL FOR..DATE..........

I AM THANKFUL FOR..DATE..........

QUOTE OR HIGHLIGHT OF THE WEEK..........................

MONTH

WEEK NO.

MONDAY

TUESDAY

WEDNESDAY

THURSDAY

FRIDAY

SATURDAY

SUNDAY

NOTES

I AM THANKFUL FOR..DATE..............

I AM THANKFUL FOR..DATE..............

I AM THANKFUL FOR..DATE..............

I AM THANKFUL FOR..DATE..............

I AM THANKFUL FOR..DATE..............

I AM THANKFUL FOR..DATE..............

QUOTE OR HIGHLIGHT OF THE WEEK

MONTH

WEEK NO.

MONDAY	TUESDAY
WEDNESDAY	THURSDAY	FRIDAY
SATURDAY	SUNDAY	NOTES

I AM THANKFUL FOR..DATE..........

I AM THANKFUL FOR..DATE..........

I AM THANKFUL FOR..DATE..........

I AM THANKFUL FOR..DATE..........

I AM THANKFUL FOR..DATE..........

I AM THANKFUL FOR..DATE..........

QUOTE OR HIGHLIGHT OF THE WEEK.........................

MONTH

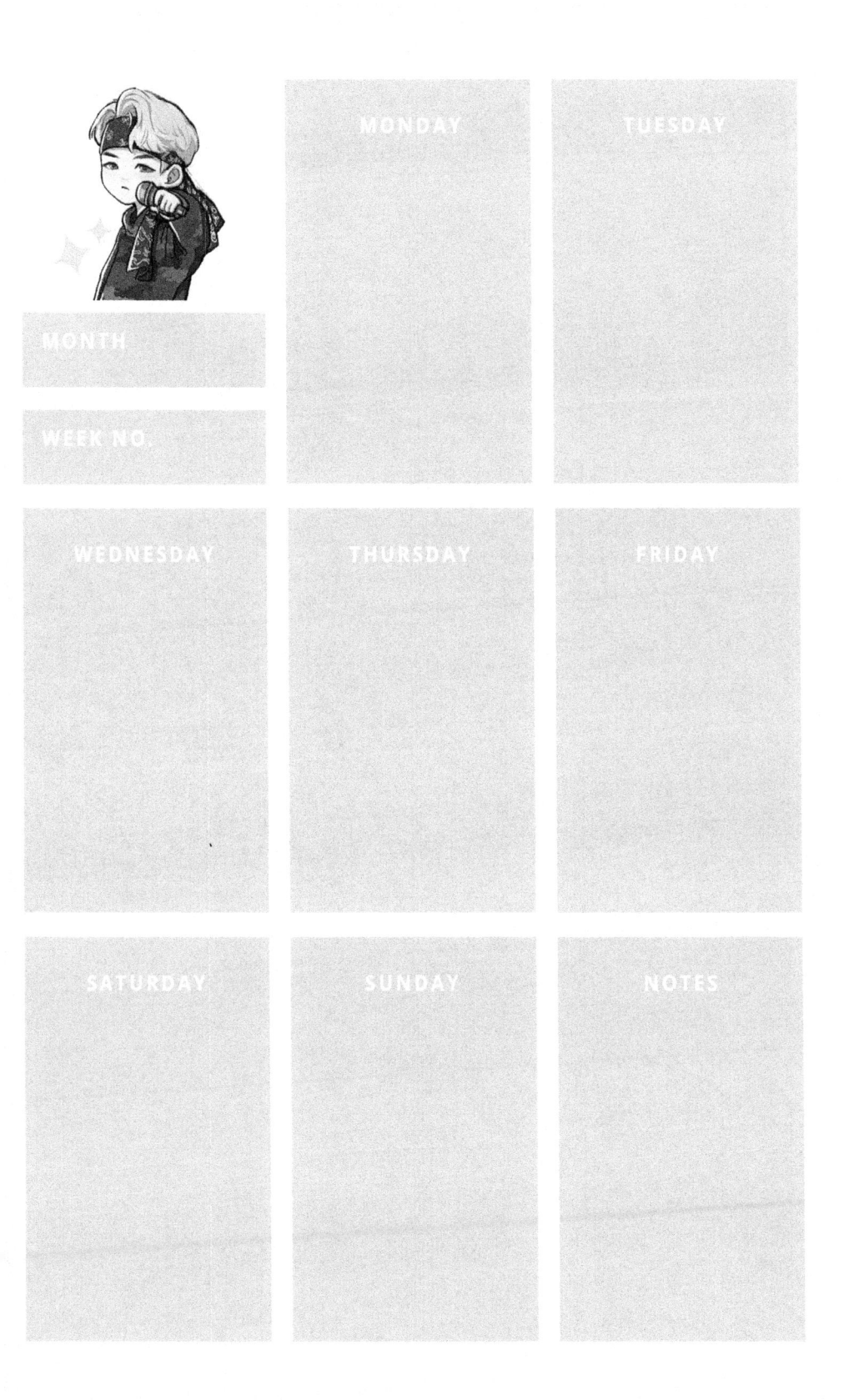

WEEK NO.

MONDAY

TUESDAY

WEDNESDAY

THURSDAY

FRIDAY

SATURDAY

SUNDAY

NOTES

| I AM THANKFUL FOR | DATE |

welcome BACK!!!

| I AM THANKFUL FOR | DATE |

| I AM THANKFUL FOR | DATE |

| I AM THANKFUL FOR | DATE |

| I AM THANKFUL FOR | DATE |

| I AM THANKFUL FOR | DATE |

QUOTE OR HIGHLIGHT OF THE WEEK

MONTH

WEEK NO.

MONDAY

TUESDAY

WEDNESDAY

THURSDAY

FRIDAY

SATURDAY

SUNDAY

NOTES

I AM THANKFUL FOR .... DATE ....

I AM THANKFUL FOR .... DATE ....

I AM THANKFUL FOR .... DATE ....

I AM THANKFUL FOR .... DATE ....

I AM THANKFUL FOR .... DATE ....

I AM THANKFUL FOR .... DATE ....

QUOTE OR HIGHLIGHT OF THE WEEK ....

MONTH

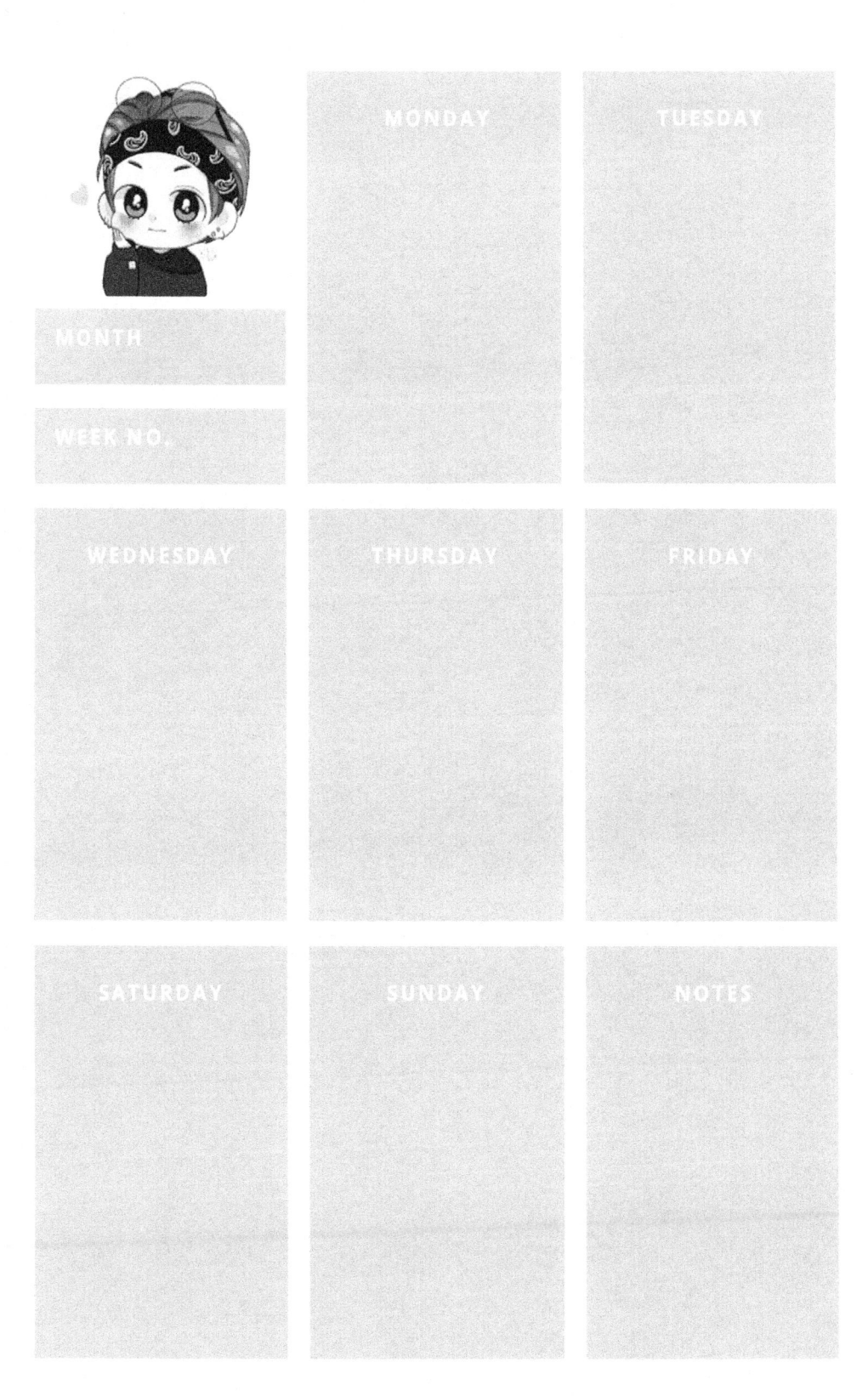

WEEK NO.

MONDAY

TUESDAY

WEDNESDAY

THURSDAY

FRIDAY

SATURDAY

SUNDAY

NOTES

| I AM THANKFUL FOR.. DATE................
....
....
| I AM THANKFUL FOR.. DATE................
....
....

| I AM THANKFUL FOR.. DATE................
....
....
| I AM THANKFUL FOR.. DATE................
....
....

| I AM THANKFUL FOR.. DATE................
....
....
| I AM THANKFUL FOR.. DATE................
....
....

QUOTE OR HIGHLIGHT OF THE WEEK..
....
....
....
....

MONTH

WEEK NO.

MONDAY

TUESDAY

WEDNESDAY

THURSDAY

FRIDAY

SATURDAY

SUNDAY

NOTES

I AM THANKFUL FOR..DATE..................
....
....

I AM THANKFUL FOR..DATE..................
....
....

I AM THANKFUL FOR..DATE..................
....
....

I AM THANKFUL FOR..DATE..................
....
....

I AM THANKFUL FOR..DATE..................
....
....

I AM THANKFUL FOR..DATE..................
....
....

QUOTE OR HIGHLIGHT OF THE WEEK...
....
....
....
....
....

MONTH

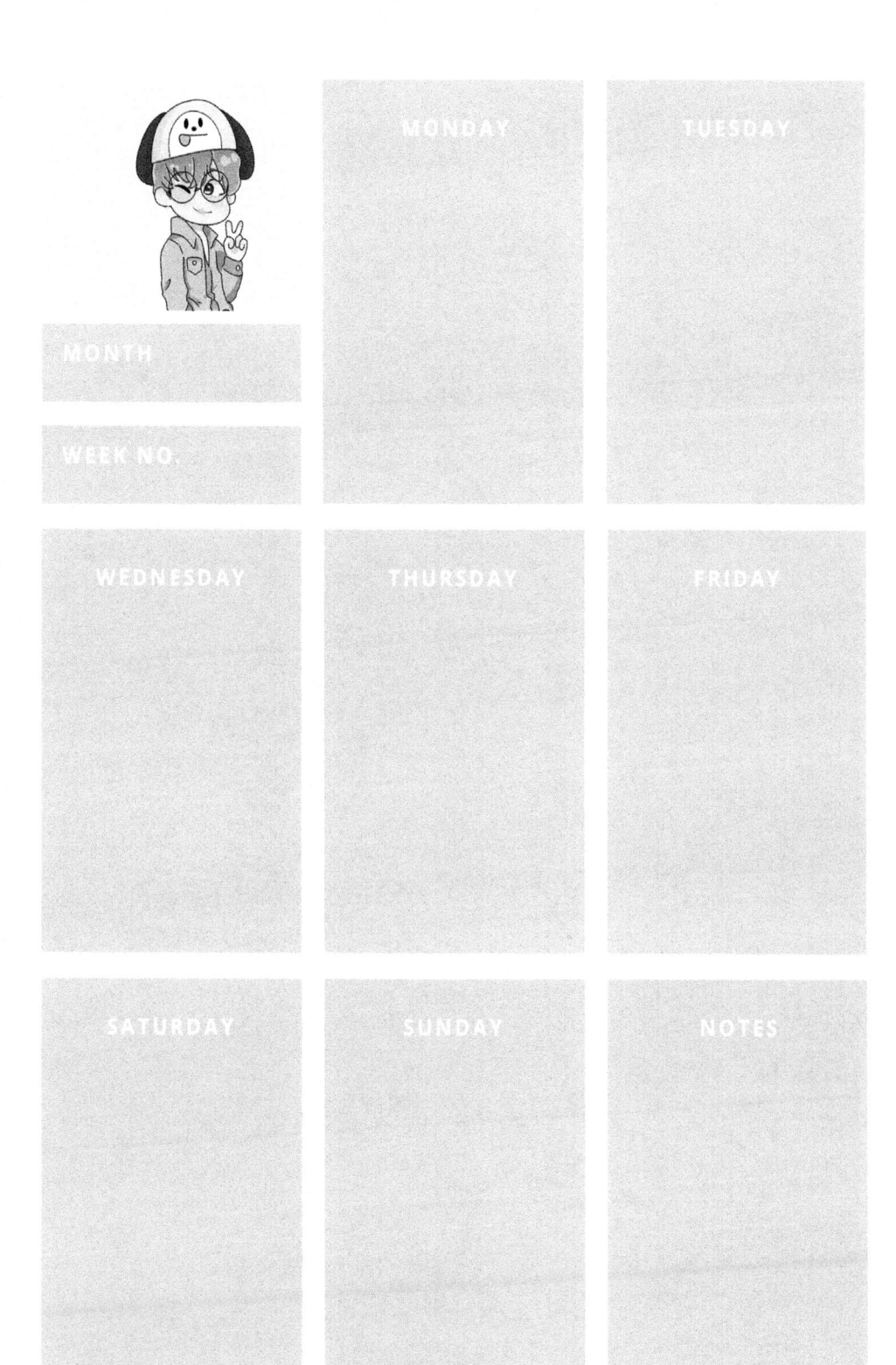

WEEK NO.

MONDAY

TUESDAY

WEDNESDAY

THURSDAY

FRIDAY

SATURDAY

SUNDAY

NOTES

I AM THANKFUL FOR..DATE...........

I AM THANKFUL FOR..DATE...........

I AM THANKFUL FOR..DATE...........

I AM THANKFUL FOR..DATE...........

I AM THANKFUL FOR..DATE...........

I AM THANKFUL FOR..DATE...........

QUOTE OR HIGHLIGHT OF THE WEEK..............................

MONTH

WEEK NO.

MONDAY

TUESDAY

WEDNESDAY

THURSDAY

FRIDAY

SATURDAY

SUNDAY

NOTES

I AM THANKFUL FOR..DATE..............
....
....
I AM THANKFUL FOR..DATE..............
....
....

I AM THANKFUL FOR..DATE..............
....
....
I AM THANKFUL FOR..DATE..............
....
....

I AM THANKFUL FOR..DATE..............
....
....
I AM THANKFUL FOR..DATE..............
....
....

QUOTE OR HIGHLIGHT OF THE WEEK...
....
....
....
BTS
....

MONTH

WEEK NO.

MONDAY	TUESDAY

WEDNESDAY	THURSDAY	FRIDAY

SATURDAY	SUNDAY	NOTES

I AM THANKFUL FOR...DATE..............

....
....

I AM THANKFUL FOR...DATE..............

....
....

I AM THANKFUL FOR...DATE..............

....
....

I AM THANKFUL FOR...DATE..............

....
....

I AM THANKFUL FOR...DATE..............

....
....

I AM THANKFUL FOR...DATE..............

....
....

QUOTE OR HIGHLIGHT OF THE WEEK..

....
....
....
....

MONTH

WEEK NO.

MONDAY

TUESDAY

WEDNESDAY

THURSDAY

FRIDAY

SATURDAY

SUNDAY

NOTES

I AM THANKFUL FOR	DATE

I AM THANKFUL FOR	DATE

I AM THANKFUL FOR	DATE

I AM THANKFUL FOR	DATE

I AM THANKFUL FOR	DATE

I AM THANKFUL FOR	DATE

QUOTE OR HIGHLIGHT OF THE WEEK

MONTH

WEEK NO.

MONDAY

TUESDAY

WEDNESDAY

THURSDAY

FRIDAY

SATURDAY

SUNDAY

NOTES

I AM THANKFUL FOR..DATE..........

I AM THANKFUL FOR..DATE..........

I AM THANKFUL FOR..DATE..........

I AM THANKFUL FOR..DATE..........

I AM THANKFUL FOR..DATE..........

I AM THANKFUL FOR..DATE..........

QUOTE OR HIGHLIGHT OF THE WEEK..

MONTH

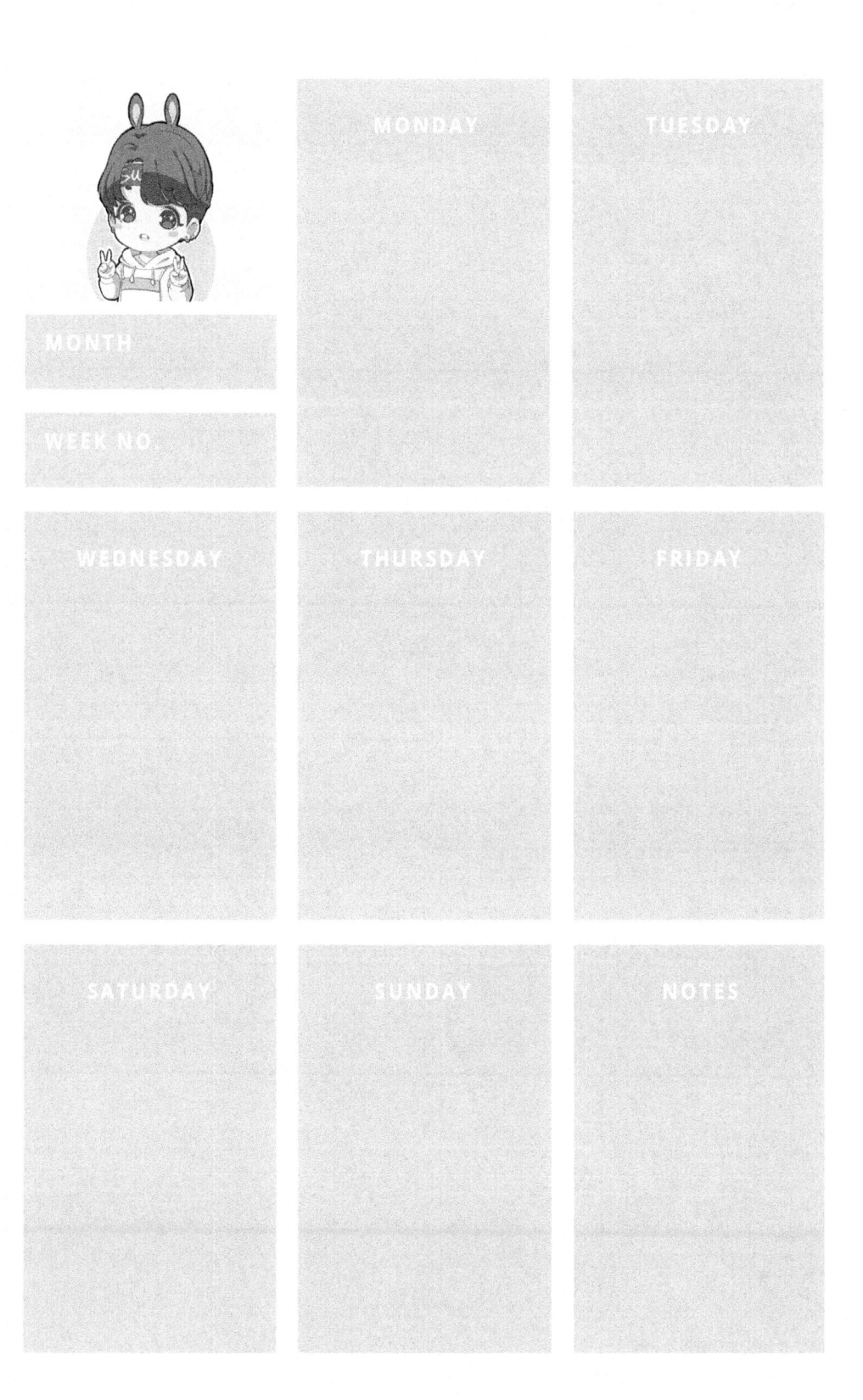

WEEK NO.

MONDAY

TUESDAY

WEDNESDAY

THURSDAY

FRIDAY

SATURDAY

SUNDAY

NOTES

I AM THANKFUL FOR...DATE......

I AM THANKFUL FOR...DATE......

I AM THANKFUL FOR...DATE......

I AM THANKFUL FOR...DATE......

I AM THANKFUL FOR...DATE......

I AM THANKFUL FOR...DATE......

QUOTE OR HIGHLIGHT OF THE WEEK

MONTH

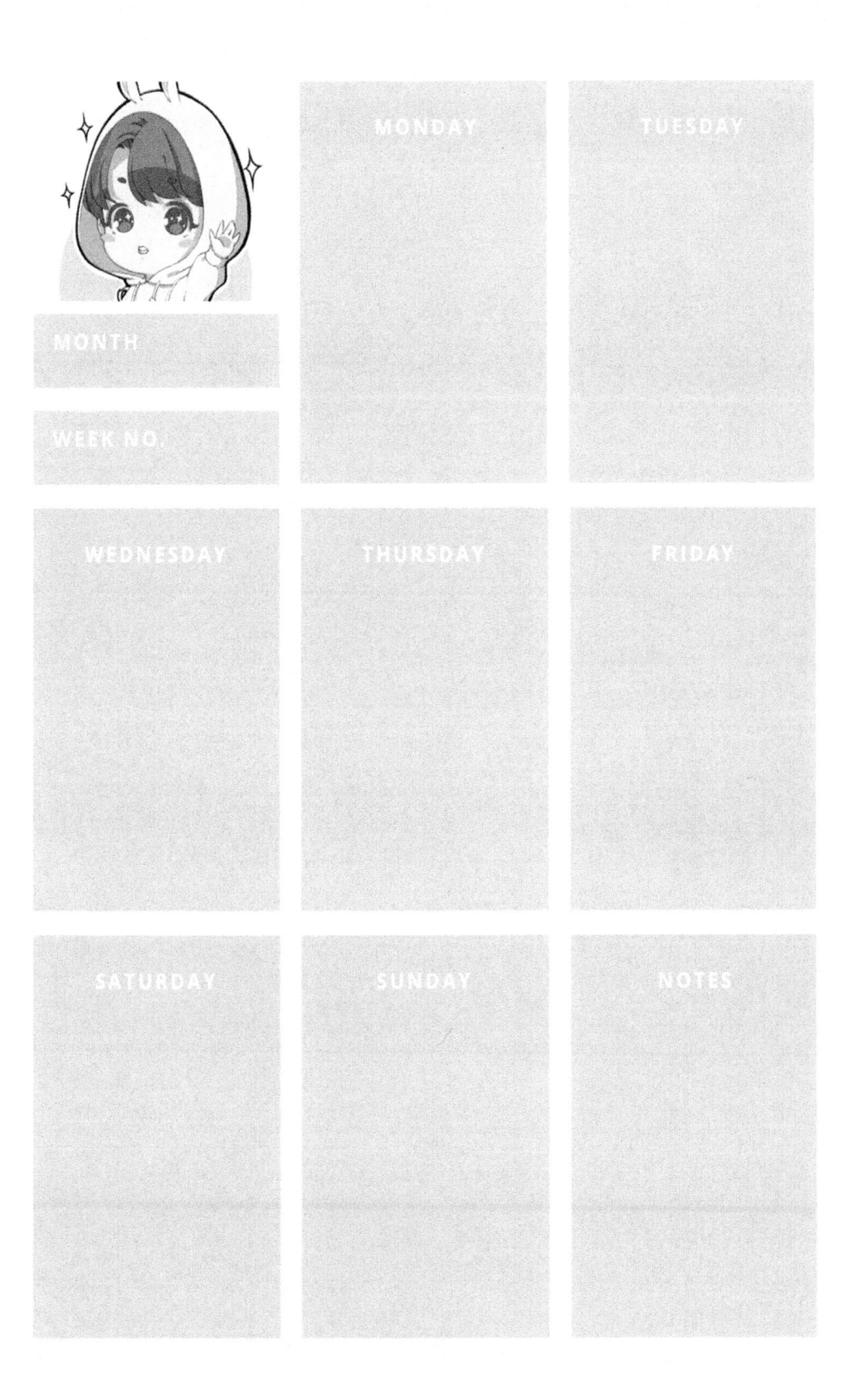

WEEK NO.

MONDAY

TUESDAY

WEDNESDAY

THURSDAY

FRIDAY

SATURDAY

SUNDAY

NOTES

I AM THANKFUL FOR.......... DATE..........

BTS ♥

I AM THANKFUL FOR.......... DATE..........

I AM THANKFUL FOR.......... DATE..........

I AM THANKFUL FOR.......... DATE..........

I AM THANKFUL FOR.......... DATE..........

I AM THANKFUL FOR.......... DATE..........

QUOTE OR HIGHLIGHT OF THE WEEK..........

MONTH

WEEK NO.

MONDAY

TUESDAY

WEDNESDAY

THURSDAY

FRIDAY

SATURDAY

SUNDAY

NOTES

I AM THANKFUL FOR	DATE

I AM THANKFUL FOR	DATE

I AM THANKFUL FOR	DATE

I AM THANKFUL FOR	DATE

I AM THANKFUL FOR	DATE

I AM THANKFUL FOR	DATE

QUOTE OR HIGHLIGHT OF THE WEEK

MONTH

WEEK NO.

MONDAY

TUESDAY

WEDNESDAY

THURSDAY

FRIDAY

SATURDAY

SUNDAY

NOTES

| I AM THANKFUL FOR | DATE |

| I AM THANKFUL FOR | DATE |

| I AM THANKFUL FOR | DATE |

| I AM THANKFUL FOR | DATE |

| I AM THANKFUL FOR | DATE |

| I AM THANKFUL FOR | DATE |

QUOTE OR HIGHLIGHT OF THE WEEK

MONTH

WEEK NO.

MONDAY

TUESDAY

WEDNESDAY

THURSDAY

FRIDAY

SATURDAY

SUNDAY

NOTES

I AM THANKFUL FOR..DATE..................

BTS ♥

I AM THANKFUL FOR..DATE..................

I AM THANKFUL FOR..DATE..................

I AM THANKFUL FOR..DATE..................

I AM THANKFUL FOR..DATE..................

I AM THANKFUL FOR..DATE..................

QUOTE OR HIGHLIGHT OF THE WEEK...............................

MONTH

WEEK NO.

MONDAY

TUESDAY

WEDNESDAY

THURSDAY

FRIDAY

SATURDAY

SUNDAY

NOTES

I AM THANKFUL FOR.. DATE..............

I AM THANKFUL FOR.. DATE..............

I AM THANKFUL FOR.. DATE..............

I AM THANKFUL FOR.. DATE..............

I AM THANKFUL FOR.. DATE..............

I AM THANKFUL FOR.. DATE..............

QUOTE OR HIGHLIGHT OF THE WEEK.............................

NOT TODAY

MONTH

WEEK NO.

MONDAY

TUESDAY

WEDNESDAY

THURSDAY

FRIDAY

SATURDAY

SUNDAY

NOTES

I AM THANKFUL FOR .... DATE ....

....

I AM THANKFUL FOR .... DATE ....

....

I AM THANKFUL FOR .... DATE ....

....

I AM THANKFUL FOR .... DATE ....

....

I AM THANKFUL FOR .... DATE ....

....

I AM THANKFUL FOR .... DATE ....

....

QUOTE OR HIGHLIGHT OF THE WEEK ....

....

MONTH

WEEK NO.

MONDAY

TUESDAY

WEDNESDAY

THURSDAY

FRIDAY

SATURDAY

SUNDAY

NOTES

I AM THANKFUL FOR..DATE............

I AM THANKFUL FOR..DATE............

I AM THANKFUL FOR..DATE............

I AM THANKFUL FOR..DATE............

I AM THANKFUL FOR..DATE............

I AM THANKFUL FOR..DATE............

QUOTE OR HIGHLIGHT OF THE WEEK..................................

TOMATO

MONTH

WEEK NO.

MONDAY

TUESDAY

WEDNESDAY

THURSDAY

FRIDAY

SATURDAY

SUNDAY

NOTES

I AM THANKFUL FOR	DATE

I AM THANKFUL FOR	DATE

I AM THANKFUL FOR	DATE

I AM THANKFUL FOR	DATE

I AM THANKFUL FOR	DATE

I AM THANKFUL FOR	DATE

QUOTE OR HIGHLIGHT OF THE WEEK

MONTH

WEEK NO.

MONDAY

TUESDAY

WEDNESDAY

THURSDAY

FRIDAY

SATURDAY

SUNDAY

NOTES

I AM THANKFUL FOR...DATE...............
....
....

I AM THANKFUL FOR...DATE...............
....
....

I AM THANKFUL FOR...DATE...............
....
....

I AM THANKFUL FOR...DATE...............
....
....

I AM THANKFUL FOR...DATE...............
....
....

I AM THANKFUL FOR...DATE...............
....
....

QUOTE OR HIGHLIGHT OF THE WEEK...
....
....
....
....

MONTH

WEEK NO.

MONDAY

TUESDAY

WEDNESDAY

THURSDAY

FRIDAY

SATURDAY

SUNDAY

NOTES

BTS

I AM THANKFUL FOR...DATE..............

I AM THANKFUL FOR...DATE..............

I AM THANKFUL FOR...DATE..............

I AM THANKFUL FOR...DATE..............

I AM THANKFUL FOR...DATE..............

I AM THANKFUL FOR...DATE..............

QUOTE OR HIGHLIGHT OF THE WEEK..

MAP OF THE SOUL
7

MONTH

WEEK NO.

MONDAY

TUESDAY

WEDNESDAY

THURSDAY

FRIDAY

SATURDAY

SUNDAY

NOTES

I AM THANKFUL FOR..DATE..............

I AM THANKFUL FOR..DATE..............

I AM THANKFUL FOR..DATE..............

I AM THANKFUL FOR..DATE..............

I AM THANKFUL FOR..DATE..............

I AM THANKFUL FOR..DATE..............

QUOTE OR HIGHLIGHT OF THE WEEK...

MONTH

WEEK NO.

MONDAY

TUESDAY

WEDNESDAY

THURSDAY

FRIDAY

SATURDAY

SUNDAY

NOTES

I AM THANKFUL FOR	DATE

I AM THANKFUL FOR	DATE

I AM THANKFUL FOR	DATE

I AM THANKFUL FOR	DATE

I AM THANKFUL FOR	DATE

I AM THANKFUL FOR	DATE

QUOTE OR HIGHLIGHT OF THE WEEK

MONTH

WEEK NO.

MONDAY

TUESDAY

WEDNESDAY

THURSDAY

FRIDAY

SATURDAY

SUNDAY

NOTES

I AM THANKFUL FOR......... DATE.........

I AM THANKFUL FOR......... DATE.........

I AM THANKFUL FOR......... DATE.........

I AM THANKFUL FOR......... DATE.........

I AM THANKFUL FOR......... DATE.........

I AM THANKFUL FOR......... DATE.........

QUOTE OR HIGHLIGHT OF THE WEEK.........

Made in the USA
Monee, IL
23 November 2020